Voices of Freedom

I Have a Dream

Karen Price Hossell

Heinemann
LIBRARY

Chicago, Illinois

© 2006 Heinemann Library
a division of Reed Elsevier, Inc.
Chicago, Illinois
Customer Service: 888-454-2279
Visit our website at www.heinemannlibrary.com

Printed and bound in Hong Kong, China by WKT Company Limited
10 09 08 07 06
10 9 8 7 6 5 4 3 2 1

Library of Congress Cataloging-in-Publication Data:
Price Hossell, Karen, 1957-
  I have a dream / Karen Price Hossell.
    p. cm. -- (Voices of freedom)
  Includes bibliographical references (p.   ) and index.
  ISBN 1-4034-6811-7 (hc) -- ISBN 1-4034-6816-8 (pb)
  1. King, Martin Luther, Jr., 1929-1968. I have a dream--Juvenile literature. 2. March on Washington for Jobs and Freedom, Washington, D.C., 1963--Juvenile literature. 3. Speeches, addresses, etc., American--Washington (D.C.)-- Juvenile literature. 4. King, Martin Luther, Jr., 1929-1968--Juvenile literature. 5. African Americans--Biography-- Juvenile literature. 6. Civil rights workers--United States--Biography--Juvenile literature. 7. African Americans--Civil rights--History--20th century--Juvenile literature. 8. Civil rights movements--United States--History--20th century-- Juvenile literature. I. Title. II. Series.
  E185.97.K5P75 2005
  323'.092--dc22

                              2005006269

Acknowledgments
The publisher would like to thank the following for permission to reproduce photographs:
Corbis pp. title, 4 both (Bettmann), 6 (Bettmann), 7 (Flip Schulke), 8, 9, 10 (Medford Historical Society Collection), 11 (Bettmann), 12 (Bettmann), 13 (Bettmann), 14 (Bettmann), 15 (Bettmann), 16 (Bettmann), 17 (Bettmann), 18 (Bettmann), 19 (Bettmann), 20 (James Randklev), 21 (Bettmann), 22 (Bettmann), 23 (Bettmann), 25 (Wally McNamee), 27 (Bettmann), 28 (Bettmann), 30 (Flip Schulke), 31 (Bettmann), 32 (Kevin Fleming), 33 (Bettmann), 34 (Bettmann), 35 (Bettmann), 36 (Bettmann), 37 (Bettmann), 38 (Flip Schulke), 39 (Flip Schulke), 40 (Flip Schulke), 41 (Bettmann), 42 (Bettmann), 43 (Flip Schulke), 44 (Dave G. Houser), 45 (Reinhard Eisele); Getty Images p. 29 (Time Magazine, copyright Time Inc./Time Life Pictures); Heinemann Library p. 5 (Jill Birschbach); Library of Congress pp. 4, 26.

Cover image of Martin Luther King Jr. reproduced with permission of Corbis (Flip Schulke).

Every effort has been made to contact copyright holders of any material reproduced in this book. Any omissions will be rectified in subsequent printings if notice is given to the publisher

Some words are shown in bold, **like this**. You can find out what they mean by looking in the glossary.

Contents

Remembering Important Events

A well-written and well-delivered speech can become an important event. The speech can have an impact on the immediate audience and on people who hear about the speech or listen to it years after it was given. Certain speeches capture the spirit of the times in which they were delivered. Quotes from these speeches are often remembered and repeated. Sometimes people know a quote from a speech but know little about the speech itself.

"Four score and seven years ago" comes from a speech Abraham Lincoln made in Gettysburg, Pennsylvania in 1863. In his speech Lincoln inspired and encouraged Americans who were suffering through the Civil War.

"The only thing we have to fear is fear itself" comes from a speech President Franklin Roosevelt made in 1933. It helped give courage to the country at a difficult time.

"Ask not what your country can do for you, but what you can do for your country" is from John Kennedy's 1961 **inauguration** address. It captured a feeling of patriotism in the United States at the time.

Over time, what people remember about a certain speech may change. One person may report the words incorrectly to another person who writes the speech down. This is why historians like to find original **drafts** of important speeches. Drafts of speeches are one kind of primary source.

The speeches of Franklin Delano Roosevelt, John F. Kennedy, and Abraham Lincoln are all part of our national vocabulary.

The collection at the Library of Congress includes 29 million books, 2.7 million recordings, 12 million photographs, and over four million maps.

Primary sources

Primary sources can include letters, diaries, articles, and other documents written by people who witnessed or were directly involved in an event. They can also include other kinds of records, such as tapes, video recordings, or photographs.

Primary sources are valuable historical records because they provide an important record of events. The United States keeps most of its important historical records in two places. One is the Library of Congress, which is in Washington, D.C. The other is the National Archives and Records Administration, or NARA. Included in these storage facilities are recordings and original manuscripts of notable speeches. One such speech is called "I Have a Dream." It was delivered in 1963 by Dr. Martin Luther King Jr.

Secondary sources

Another category of sources are those written by people who have studied primary sources. These are secondary sources. Scholars study these and write their own books and articles based on their research. When you write a research paper for school you are creating a secondary source. However, if in the future someone wants to study how students wrote research papers in the 21st Century, your paper could become a primary source.

What Is "I Have a Dream"?

On August 28, 1963, about 250,000 people marched from the Washington Monument to the Lincoln Memorial in Washington, D.C. They marched in protest, and they marched to show support for one another and the cause of **civil rights**.

Even though the March on Washington was a protest march, it was peaceful. Police officers lined the streets, waiting for the violence they thought might happen. Other marches similar to this one had been violent. They thought this one would be, too.

At the Lincoln Memorial people gathered to hear a program that included musical performers, movie stars, and religious and civil rights leaders.

Martin Luther King Jr.

One of the civil rights leaders who spoke that day was Martin Luther King Jr. King's influence was one reason the march was so peaceful. He believed in changing wrongs through nonviolence. His reputation was already strong throughout the organizations that fought for civil rights. But after his speech that day, King would become the leader of the American civil rights movement.

The speech King made on that historic day is called "I Have a Dream." King was a Baptist minister and had spoken before crowds, both large and small, before. He had a strong presence, and he knew how to make people listen. Because the speech was televised, he spoke not only to the crowd of a quarter-million people in Washington, D.C., but also to millions around the world.

The large crowd waits for the March on Washington ceremonies to begin.

"I Have a Dream" was delivered from the steps of the Lincoln Memorial in honor of Lincoln's role in ending slavery.

Slavery

To understand what the civil rights movement and King's "I Have a Dream" speech are all about, it is important to understand a little bit about the history of African Americans in the United States.

The first slave ship landed in the American colonies in 1619. It carried hundreds of Africans who had been kidnapped from their homes.

For the next 200 years, the number of slaves in the American colonies grew. In 1808 **Congress** passed a law that made buying and selling slaves that came from outside the United States illegal. But that did not end slavery, because every child born to a slave already in the United States was automatically a slave.

King's primary sources

In 2003 King's wife and children decided to put King's papers and books up for auction, or public sale. They presented the collection to an auction house in New York City called Sotheby's. Included in the collection were papers King wrote in high school and college, books he owned, and an early copy of "I Have a Dream." The Kings did not want the collection divided; they wanted one person or organization to purchase the entire group of works. Sotheby's estimated that the papers were worth $30 million.

The End of Slavery

Some Americans thought there was nothing wrong with owning slaves. They believed that black people and white people were not equal, and that whites had the right to control and enslave blacks. But some Americans, called **abolitionists**, believed strongly that slavery was wrong and that it should end. In the 1800s they became more vocal about their beliefs. As the century continued, they began to hold rallies and publish newspapers and pamphlets about the evils of slavery.

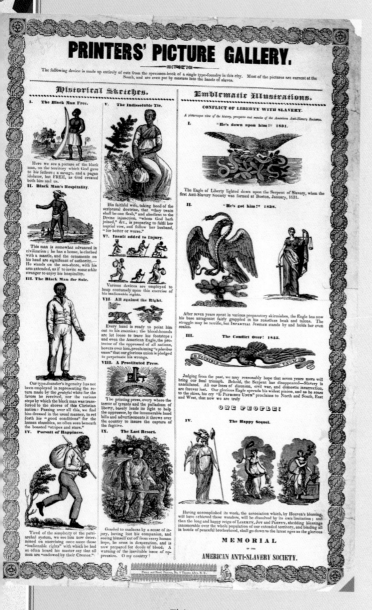

This pamphlet was put out by an abolitionist group in 1838.

States' rights

In 1803, when Thomas Jefferson was president, the United States bought a huge amount of land from France. This was called the Louisiana Purchase. This land covered much of what is now the western United States.

Soon, the United States government divided the western land into territories. **Congress** debated about whether to allow slavery in the territories. Abolitionists said slavery should not be allowed, but others believed that those who lived in the territories should decide for themselves whether to allow slavery. They worried that if slavery was outlawed in territories, it could soon be outlawed in states. Supporters of slavery started talking about "states' rights," which meant that the states had the right to make laws for themselves. They felt the **federal** government had too much power over states and made too many laws that states had to follow.

When Abraham Lincoln was elected president in 1860, states' rights supporters feared he would extend his power to the states. They already knew that Lincoln wanted slavery outlawed—maybe not immediately, but they knew he would work toward getting rid of slavery. The states in the south felt so strongly that they should have the final say in governing themselves that they decided they could not be a part of the United States with Lincoln as president. These states left the United States, also called the Union. The southern states called themselves the Confederacy and elected their own president, Jefferson Davis. In 1861 the Civil War between the Union and the Confederacy began.

The Emancipation Proclamation

Two years into the war, President Lincoln wrote the Emancipation Proclamation, which declared all slaves in the southern states free. In 1865 the war ended and the southern states were brought back into the Union. The southern states had lost their fight for states' rights and for the continuation of slavery. With the end of the war, slavery was illegal, and all slaves in the United States were free.

This illustration of the Ku Klux Klan is from 1868.

The Ku Klux Klan

In 1866 former Southern Civil War veterans in Tennessee formed The Ku Klux Klan. The Klan started as a social club, but soon its members began harassing—even killing—blacks. In 1868 the Klan killed nearly 1,000 people in Louisiana alone. In the 1920s, when more and more immigrants were coming to the United States, the Klan became popular again. They elected their members to political office and enforced **segregation** in some parts of the South. The Klan continues today, although it is not nearly as powerful as it once was.

Jim Crow Laws

When the Civil War ended, **Congress** sent military troops to the states that had rejoined the Union. The troops were to make sure the freed slaves were not mistreated and the states followed the law and did not consider leaving the union again.

Reconstruction

The period of time that the troops were in the south was called Reconstruction. Much destruction had occurred in the southern states during the war, and Reconstruction was a time for them to rebuild. Cities such as Atlanta, Georgia, and Richmond, Virginia, had been burned by the Union Army. The army also burned down or destroyed plantation homes and crops.

Charleston, South Carolina was heavily damaged during the Civil War.

During Reconstruction, former slaves had to find a way to survive. Before, most worked as field hands or in homes of plantations owners as maids, cooks, butlers, and drivers. Many continued to do the same work after the war, but this time for money. Some blacks ran for political office and were elected into positions of power, where they could have a part in making laws. Reconstruction was a promising time for former slaves, who were finally beginning to gain **civil rights**.

Jim Crow laws

By 1877 Congress had decided that **federal** troops could leave the South to rule itself. Once the troops were gone, southern whites began to find ways to separate themselves from blacks. They saw that blacks were gaining power in business and in politics, and many whites did not like this. Blacks, they thought, did not deserve to have the same rights as whites. So whites began to make laws that took away the rights of black people. These were called Jim Crow Laws. Jim Crow was a black character in traveling shows that were popular during the 1800s, called minstrel shows. Many of the laws resulted in African Americans being treated no better than when they were slaves.

Some of the laws were not written laws, but widely held beliefs. For example, blacks were expected to be polite to whites at all times, no matter how badly white people treated them. Black men had to take off their hats in the presence of white people. And when they were asked into the home of a white person, black people were expected to enter only through the back door.

T.D. Rice, shown here, is credited as the creator of Jim Crow.

The goal of the laws that were actually passed by state **legislatures** was to keep the races apart. In restaurants blacks and whites could not eat in the same dining room. Blacks had separate hotels, water fountains, and schools. On public transportation such as buses and trains, they were expected to give up their seats to whites. In the south, blacks and whites did nearly everything separately.

Plessy vs. Ferguson

In 1892 the system that blacks had to be separate from whites was challenged by Homer Plessy. He boarded a train in Louisiana and sat in a car designated for whites, even though he was part black. Plessy refused to move and was arrested. The case went all the way to the United States **Supreme Court**, which decided that the separation of races did not violate the United States Constitution. The court found that since both races had equal facilities, the law that separated them was fair. This idea is known as "separate but equal."

The Early Civil Rights Movement

As the 1900s began, the idea of "separate but equal" continued. Blacks and whites might sometimes work together or fight together in wars, but most of the time they did things separately. As the twentieth century continued, however, more people began to question the fairness of this way of living.

Brown vs. Board of Education

In 1952 the United States **Supreme Court** first heard the case of *Brown vs. Board of Education*. In the court case, a young black girl was forced to attend a school that was far from her home. A school for white children was just down the road, but she had to board a bus and travel for miles to get to an all-black school. The National Association for the Advancement of Colored People (NAACP), decided to sue her local school board. The NAACP claimed this was not equal treatment because she had to go so far, while white students in her neighborhood walked only a few blocks to school. The Supreme Court agreed with the NAACP. They said that the child should not have to travel such a distance just because of the color of her skin. The court said that **segregation** in education was unconstitutional because separate schools were unequal.

The NAACP

The National Association for the Advancement of Colored People was founded in 1908 after a race riot in Springfield, Illinois. Most of the original members were whites who were concerned that blacks were not being treated fairly or legally. The primary goal of the group was to make sure that amendments to the constitution passed by Congress during and after the Civil War, were followed. The amendments ensured an end to slavery, equal protection for everyone under the law, and the right of all men to vote (women did not have the right to vote in the United States until 1920). The NAACP worked toward this goal by bringing violations of the amendments to court. Later, the NAACP became involved with other issues, including the concerns of black workers that they were not being treated justly.

This decision meant that now African Americans had the right to go to the same schools whites attended if they wished. The decision in *Brown vs. Board of Education* did not end segregation in all public areas, such as restrooms and restaurants. However, once the ruling had been made pressure was put on all forms of state supported segregation.

Justice Thurgood Marshall

Thurgood Marshall was born in 1908 and graduated from Howard University with a law degree in 1933. He became chief counsel, or the primary attorney, for the NAACP. In that role, he argued more than thirty cases before the United States Supreme Court about racial segregation. Perhaps the most important case he handled was *Brown vs. Board of Education*. In 1964 President Lyndon B. Johnson appointed Marshall to the United States Supreme Court. He was the first African American on the nation's highest court. Marshall retired in 1991 and died in 1993.

Know It!

The United States Supreme Court is the highest court in the land. This means that it has the power to overturn rulings by other courts. If someone disagrees with a decision made by another court, they can ask the Supreme Court to listen to their argument. The Supreme Court does not agree to listen to all cases. The court is made up of nine justices. The justices are appointed by the president of the United States and once appointed serve for the rest of their lives, or until they resign.

Thurgood Marshall in 1958 outside of the Supreme Court building.

Fighting Jim Crow

In some places, the move toward ending **segregation** came slowly. The situation was highlighted on December 1, 1955, in Montgomery, Alabama. Rosa Parks had worked a long day as a seamstress, and she was tired. She boarded a bus for home and sat down. Soon, the bus became crowded, and whites had to stand in the aisle. The bus driver told Parks, along with other blacks, that they had to stand up and let the white people sit down.

Rosa Parks, a year after her arrest for refusing to give up her seat on the bus.

Because she refused to give up her seat, Rosa Parks was arrested. When the news spread, many people gathered to support her, including Martin Luther King. At the time, King was only 26. But the idea of blacks receiving the treatment and the rights they deserved was important to him. By the time that meeting in Montgomery was over, King and another man, Rev. Ralph Abernathy, had been chosen to lead a new group called Montgomery in Action, or MIA.

Bus boycott

The group realized that most of the people who rode buses in Montgomery were black. They decided to show businesspeople how much money would be lost in just one day if blacks stopped riding the bus, so they **boycotted** city buses for one day.

MIA members then asked city leaders to let blacks sit wherever they wanted on buses and to tell bus drivers they had to be polite to blacks. The leaders refused, so the boycott continued for more than a year. Blacks walked to work, and sometimes their actions so angered whites that they beat them. Someone even bombed King's home.

A Montgomery City bus sits empty during the boycott.

Many blacks became so angry about the violence that they wanted to fight back. But Martin Luther King did not believe in violence, and he encouraged people to respond to violence with peace.

As the long boycott continued, white business owners began to lose money, because blacks were not coming into town to make purchases. The bus company lost money, too, and even had King and his followers arrested, saying they were trying to ruin the bus company. King was found guilty and had to pay a $500 fine.

Under King's leadership, the MIA decided to file lawsuits against the city, charging it with segregation. The **Supreme Court** agreed that Montgomery was practicing segregation, and told city leaders they had to allow blacks to sit anywhere they wanted on the bus. This was one of the first times African Americans joined together in large numbers to stage a nonviolent protest. But it would not be the last time.

Respectful names

Over time the ways in which we refer to groups of people often change. For example, people who live on the continent of Asia were once called "Orientals" instead of "Asians." In Martin Luther King Jr.'s time the words "Negro" and "colored" were both considered respectful ways of referring to African Americans. In the 1970s the word "black" became more accepted. Today, most people prefer to use either "black" or "African American."

School Integration

Martin Luther King's leadership role in the Montgomery bus **boycott** brought him to the attention of **civil rights** workers everywhere. Many groups asked him to speak about his views about how to fight Jim Crow laws.

They needed to do this because even though the Supreme Court had declared that **segregation** was illegal, it continued, especially in the Deep South. In states such as Alabama and Mississippi, blacks and whites continued to attend separate schools. Most southern politicians allowed this to continue because, like the people they represented, they did not believe in **integration**.

Integration in Little Rock

In May of 1955, the **Supreme Court** announced that school districts must begin to integrate their schools. Still, many Americans fought against this idea. One of the most well-known examples of resistance occurred at the beginning of the 1957 school year in Little Rock, Arkansas. The local school board decided to begin integrating its schools, starting with the all-white Central High School. The governor thought there would be violence on the first day of school, so he ordered National Guard troops to go to the school. As the day grew closer, white segregationists did everything they could think of to keep blacks out of Central High. But on September 4, nine black students arrived to start the new school year. They were greeted by a crowd of angry protestors who screamed, cursed, and spit at them.

African-American students being escorted by soldiers into Little Rock High School.

LITTLE ROCK CENTR

Jefferson Thomas, one of the first black students at Little Rock Central High, waits alone for a bus home.

Elizabeth Eckford was the first black person to try to walk into the school. She was frightened as guards escorted her through the crowd. Later, she said that the guards did little to protect her, and the crowd shouted "**Lynch** her!" The crowd became so violent that the black students did not enter the school.

Violence

On September 23, after a judge reviewed the situation, the students again returned to the school, this time with police escorts. Once more they were greeted by an angry crowd of white segregationists. After the students went into the school, the mob turned on journalists, both black and white, who were covering the story for newspapers and television. The next day, a larger mob of people came to the school, shouting and threatening violence. The black students were given personal bodyguards, and **federal** troops were stationed inside the school for the entire school year.

The violence and **racism** in Little Rock was shown on television not only across the United States, but all over the world. People in other countries were often surprised to learn that there was so much hatred and lack of understanding in what was supposed to be the land of freedom.

Sit-Ins and Freedom Rides

African Americans continued to fight for their rights. In February 1960 a group of black college students decided to sit at an all-white lunch counter in Greensboro, North Carolina. In North Carolina rules about **segregation** were still enforced.

Sit-ins

The students were told to move, and they refused. They sat at the counter until closing time and went back the next day, this time with nineteen other black students. Again management refused to serve them, and the students remained until closing time. This kind of protest became known as a sit-in. By the end of the week, 400 college students had joined the sit-in, each taking his or her turn sitting at the counter. By the end of 1961, thousands of people fought for their rights by staging sit-ins in restaurants, libraries, swimming pools, and other public areas.

The fight for **civil rights** continued. More cases involving segregation went to the United States **Supreme Court**, and each time the court declared that any segregation was illegal.

Four college students sit at the Woolworth's lunch counter in North Carolina.

This Freedom Rider's bus was burned by a white mob.

Freedom Riders

One kind of segregation blacks decided to test was at railroad and bus station rest areas and restrooms. In May 1961 a group of young people, both black and white, boarded two buses in Washington, D.C. and headed south. Calling their trip the Freedom Ride, they planned to make stops at bus stations to make sure segregation had ended there. The farther south they traveled, the more resistance they encountered. A mob in Alabama slashed the tires on one of the buses, and later another mob broke the windows and threw a firebomb into the bus. Eventually, the violence became so bad that the bus drivers refused to continue, so the ride ended. But hundreds of Americans decided to continue the ride for them, coming to Birmingham, Alabama, in support of the cause.

The larger group of riders continued the ride to Montgomery, where they were greeted by at least 1,000 rioting whites, who beat the riders. As the violence continued for several days, President Kennedy sent **federal** troops to the area. The troops asked the Freedom Riders to end their journey, fearing more violence. But the riders were determined to continue their fight for civil rights. Eventually, the ride resulted in ending segregation in southern bus station restrooms and waiting rooms.

The next large protest occurred in 1963 in Birmingham, Alabama, where Jim Crow laws were still in effect. While Martin Luther King Jr. was already a well-known civil rights leader, his actions in Birmingham would make him known all over the world.

Martin Luther King Jr.

Martin Luther King Jr. was born in Atlanta, Georgia, in 1929. He graduated from Morehouse College in 1948 and became a Baptist minister the same year. In 1951, he graduated from seminary (a school that educates ministers and preachers), and in 1953 he married Coretta Scott. King became the pastor of the Dexter Avenue Baptist Church in 1954, and a year later he received a doctoral degree from Boston.

The home where Martin Luther King was born is now part of a national historic site.

Fighting segregation

In 1963 in Birmingham, Alabama police chief Eugene "Bull" Connor decided that rather than **desegregating** city facilities, such as parks, playgrounds, and golf courses, he would close them. He also enforced Jim Crow laws in restaurants, theaters, and other public places.

King, along with other **civil rights** leaders, led peaceful marches in the spring of 1963 to protest these practices. They also staged **boycotts** and sit-ins. Connor arrested many of the protestors, including King.

Later, however, the protests resulted in violence. One night, a large group of schoolchildren decided to march peacefully through the streets of Birmingham. At first, civil rights leaders tried to discourage them, but then decided the march could go on. Police attacked the marchers by spraying them with fire hoses, tear gas, and attack dogs. Because the march was televised on American news, millions of people saw the attacks.

President Kennedy sent some of his staff to Birmingham to oversee a negotiation between blacks and whites. Blacks agreed that the protests would stop, and whites agreed to allow **integration**. But the Ku Klux Klan and other **racists** were angered by the agreement and bombed the home of King's brother and a black-only hotel. Reacting to the bombings, some blacks began rioting and set fire to white-owned businesses. Thousands of **federal** troops then entered the city to enforce order.

These schoolchildren are being arrested after participating in a peaceful civil rights march in Birmingham.

Harry and Harriette Moore

On Christmas Day in 1951, a bomb exploded under a home in the small town of Mims, Florida. The home belonged to Harry and Harriette Moore, a married African-American couple. Mr. Moore founded the local branch of the NAACP and traveled throughout Florida, trying to start more branches. Mrs. Moore was a teacher in a tiny school for black children. Besides being Christmas Day, December 25, 1951, was also the Moore's twenty-fifth wedding anniversary.

The bomb went off under the Moore's bedroom, where they were sleeping, and blew their bed through the ceiling. Mrs. Moore's brothers lived nearby and rushed to help. They had to drive the Moores to the hospital because no local ambulance would take blacks. Mr. Moore died on the way, and Mrs. Moore died nine days later, but not before being questioned repeatedly by the FBI. At Mr. Moore's funeral flowers had to be delivered from Miami because no local florist would deliver to a black funeral. The Moore's murderers were never found, although authorities have suspected for years that the bomb was the work of the Ku Klux Klan.

The Moores are just one example of the terrible price people paid to fight for civil rights.

The Practice of Nonviolence

When King was a freshman in college he read Henry David Thoreau's *Essay on Civil Disobedience*. Thoreau wrote this essay in 1849 after spending a night in jail because he refused to pay a tax to support the Mexican War. Thoreau was a famous **abolitionist** and writer. In his essay he argued that if a person believes his or her government is doing something wrong, the person must disobey the government. Thoreau believed people should resist in a peaceful manner. His decision to go to jail rather than pay a tax is an example of resisting a law in a peaceful manner.

King was so interested in Thoreau's ideas about how to resist a bad system that he read the essay several times. King continued to study and think about nonviolence when he went to seminary. He wanted to try and find a way that nonviolence and love could help make social changes.

Nonviolence in action

In 1950 King heard a speech given by the president of Howard University (an historically black university), Dr. Mordecai Johnson. Johnson had recently gone to India and he spoke about the life of Mohandas (or Mahatma) Gandhi. Gandhi had also read Thoreau's essay and used the idea of nonviolence to help free India from British colonial rule. For King, the ideas of nonviolence agreed with his ideas about Christianity and love.

The writer Henry David Thoreau is best known for his book *Walden*.

King began studying Gandhi and urged African Americans to commit to a life of nonviolence. He understood that some people would not be able to do this and he urged those people to at least see that nonviolence could be a powerful weapon against **racism** and **discrimination**. King stressed that meeting violence with violence would only result in more violence. He believed that nonviolence was "the only morally and practically sound method open to oppressed people in their struggle for freedom." King believed that if you practiced nonviolent resistance, you had to be willing to suffer for your beliefs. This meant that if you were arrested while on a protest march, you could not try and fight the police officers. The 1963 marches in Birmingham are an example of King using his principals of nonviolence.

Some people disagreed with King's ideas about nonviolence. These people believed that the method was too slow and that change in society would only come if individual people were forced to change their behavior. They believed it was alright to use any means necessary, even violence to achieve the right outcome.

Gandhi ran a succesful campaign of nonviolence against British rule in India.

Mohandas Gandhi

Mohandas Gandhi (1869–1948) was born in India during British colonial rule. As a young man he went to England to become a lawyer. At the age of twenty-two he moved to South Africa to practice law. At the time, South Africa had a system of racial prejudice known as apartheid. This system kept different races apart and was very cruel to anyone who wasn't considered white. It was while in South Africa that Gandhi began working for racial justice.

In his forties, Gandhi returned to India to work for Indian independence from England. His principles of nonviolent resistance often led to him being arrested, but he was ultimately successful. In 1948 he was **assassinated** on his way to prayers. Gandhi is known by the name "Mahatma," which means "great soul" in Hindi.

The March on Washington

As the battle over **civil rights** continued, President John F. Kennedy knew he had to take action. Before he became president, ensuring civil rights had been one of his goals. As the civil rights movement grew Kennedy drafted a civil rights act and sent it to **Congress**. To show support for the act, civil rights leaders organized an event they called the March on Washington.

The march took place on August 28, 1963. More than 250,000 took part in the peaceful demonstration. They marched from the Washington Monument to the Lincoln Memorial. There, the huge crowd listened to speeches by civil rights leaders and performances by well-known artists of the time. The speech most remembered on that day was called "I Have a Dream," and it was delivered by King.

A poetic speech

"I Have a Dream" is considered one of the best American speeches. It is poetic, filled with imagery and figures of speech. But the words are only part of what makes the speech great. King's delivery was masterful. He spoke with passion, and he conveyed that passion to the crowd, inspiring both the audience in Washington, and the audience who watched the speech on television, to imagine a future without **racism**.

Program planners asked that each speaker take no longer than eight minutes. But King's speech lasted nineteen minutes. One reason he went so long is that he was the last speaker. Several people who helped to plan the program said the other speakers did not want to be scheduled after King. They knew that King was such a good speaker that the audience would leave after his speech, not caring who came next. Another reason was that while he had written a speech to give, while he was speaking he decided to change the speech.

Writing the speech

In King's autobiography, he explained he had arrived in Washington the night before the march. He had already thought about and sketched out some ideas about the speech. Late that evening in his hotel room he outlined his new ideas for the speech and then wrote the text of the speech. He finished, he said, at 4 a.m. on August 28.

When he delivered the speech, King followed his written version at first. But he said that the audience's reaction inspired him, and "all of a sudden this thing came to me." He had used the phrase "I have a dream" in a speech in Detroit a few months earlier. The phrase came to him on that warm day in August, and after he spoke the words he continued with that theme. "I just turned aside from the manuscript altogether," he wrote, "and didn't come back to it."

This photo, taken from the air, shows the large crowd at the March on Washington. At the time, the march was the largest political demonstration ever held in Washington.

The Speech

King begins his speech by referring to another great speech called "The Gettysburg Address." That speech was delivered by Abraham Lincoln 100 years earlier, in 1863. Lincoln is the president who freed the slaves during and after the Civil War. In these first lines, King said:

> *Five score years ago, a great American, in whose symbolic shadow we stand signed the Emancipation Proclamation. This momentous decree [order] came as a great beacon light of hope to millions of Negro slaves who had been seared [burned] in the flames of withering injustice. It came as a joyous daybreak to end the long night of captivity. But one hundred years later, we must face the tragic fact that the Negro is still not free.*

Lincoln's speech began "four score and twenty years ago"— King's begins with "five score years ago." A score is twenty years. The Emancipation Proclamation was the document Lincoln signed freeing most American slaves. But, as King said, 100 years after that document was signed, African Americans are still not really free. King went on to say:

A draft of the Emancipation Proclamation, ending slavery in the South.

> *One hundred years later, the life of the Negro is still sadly crippled by the manacles of **segregation** and the chains of **discrimination**. One hundred years later, the Negro lives on a lonely island of poverty in the midst of a vast ocean of material prosperity One hundred years later, the Negro is still languishing [growing weak] in the corners of American society and finds himself an exile in his own land.*

Know It!

King used several metaphors in his speech. A metaphor is a figure of speech where one word is used in place of another to make a comparison.

King is wearing one of the official March buttons. The buttons sold for 25 cents each.

"Chains and manacles" are used as metaphors here, referring to the actual chains and manacles worn by slaves. King used more metaphors when he provides the imagery of an "island of poverty in the midst of a vast ocean of material prosperity."

Banking metaphor

Next, King used language that refers to cashing a check at a bank. He said:

So we have come here today to dramatize an appalling condition. In a sense we have come to our nation's capital to cash a check. When the architects [writers] of our republic wrote the magnificent words of the Constitution and the Declaration of Independence, they were signing a promissory note to which every American was to fall heir.

A promissory note is a piece of paper someone signs promising that they owe something to someone else. King means here that the United States Constitution and the Declaration of Independence promised freedom to all Americans. Now, he said, blacks are ready to cash in on the promise of freedom given in those documents.

27

Insufficient Funds

As King continued his speech, he spoke more about cashing in a check, or promissory note.

This note was a promise that all men would be guaranteed the inalienable [guaranteed] rights of life, liberty, and the pursuit of happiness. It is obvious today that America has defaulted on this promissory note insofar as her citizens of color are concerned. Instead of honoring this sacred obligation [promise], America has given the Negro people a bad check which has come back marked "insufficient [not enough] funds." But we refuse to believe that the bank of justice is bankrupt [unable to pay]. We refuse to believe that there are insufficient funds in the great vaults of opportunity of this nation.

The phrase "life, liberty, and the pursuit of happiness" is taken directly from the Declaration of Independence. The author of that document, Thomas Jefferson, stated that those were rights that belonged to everyone. But, as King points out next, some Americans are refused those rights. "Insufficient funds" is more banking language—if someone does not have enough money in their bank account to cover a check, the bank says there are insufficient funds.

Ending racism

King continues with the banking metaphor in the next paragraph and spoke about ending **racism** when he said, *"Now is the time to rise from the dark and desolate valley of **segregation** to the sunlit path of racial justice."* In the next paragraph, he describes how determined African Americans are to achieve their goal, saying, *"Those who hope that the Negro needed to blow off steam and will now be content will have a rude awakening if the nation returns to business as usual. There will be neither rest nor tranquility [peace] in America until the Negro is granted his citizenship rights."*

Thomas Jefferson, one of the writers of the Delcaration of Independence, owned slaves.

In 1963 *Time* magazine chose Martin Luther King Jr. as Man of the Year for his work in the civil rights movement.

Then he tells blacks not to distrust all white people: " .... *many of our white brothers, as evidenced by their presence here today, have come to realize that their destiny [future] is tied up with our destiny and their freedom is inextricably bound to our freedom.*"

King continued to use poetic language when he said:

We can never be satisfied as long as a Negro in Mississippi cannot vote and a Negro in New York believes he has nothing for which to vote. No, no, we are not satisfied, and we will not be satisfied until justice rolls down like waters and righteousness like a mighty stream.

The Dream

Next, King challenges those who came to the March on Washington to take action and to:

Go back to Mississippi, go back to Alabama, go back to Georgia, go back to Louisiana, go back to the slums and ghettos of our northern cities, knowing that somehow this situation can and will be changed. Let us not wallow [stumble] in the valley of despair. I say to you today, my friends, that in spite of the difficulties and frustrations of the moment, I still have a dream. It is a dream deeply rooted in the American dream.

King's dream

In those last two lines, King begins the most famous section of the speech. He refers to a dream "deeply rooted in the American dream." The American dream is to have a life of freedom and happiness.

King continues to speak about the dream in the next paragraph. He quotes from the Declaration of Independence when he says, *"I have a dream that one day this nation will rise up and live out the true meaning of its creed [statement of belief]: 'We hold these truths to be self-evident: that all men are created equal.'"*

Then he goes on to say:

I have a dream that one day on the red hills of Georgia the sons of former slaves and the sons of former slaveowners will be able to sit down together at a table of brotherhood.

Three years after the March on Washington King participated in the March Against Fear in Mississippi.

*I have a dream
that one day even the state of
Mississippi, a desert state,
sweltering with the heat of
injustice and oppression, will be
transformed into an oasis
[paradise] of freedom and
justice. I have a dream that my
four children will one day live
in a nation where they will not
be judged by the color of their
skin but by the content of their
character. I have a dream today.*

King refers to Alabama's governor at the time, George Wallace, who fought against **civil rights** for blacks in the next paragraph:

*I have a dream that one day
the state of Alabama, whose
governor's lips are presently
dripping with the words of
interposition and nullification*
[words that refer to stopping
progress], *will be transformed
into a situation where little
black boys and black girls will
be able to join hands with
little white boys and white girls
and walk together as sisters
and brothers.*

George Wallace at the time of the March on Washington.

He next uses phrases from the book of Isaiah in the Bible when he says the following:

I have a dream that one day every valley shall be exalted, every hill and mountain shall be made low, the rough places will be made plain, and the crooked places will be made straight, and the glory of the Lord shall be revealed, and all flesh shall see it together. This is our hope. This is the faith with which I return to the South.

Let Freedom Ring

King concludes his speech by using lines from the song "My Country 'Tis of Thee."

This will be the day when all of God's children will be able to sing with a new meaning, 'My country, 'tis of thee, sweet land of liberty, of thee I sing. Land where my fathers died, land of the pilgrim's pride, from every mountainside, let freedom ring.' And if America is to be a great nation, this must become true.

In the next section, he repeats the phrase "let freedom ring." Repeating phrases, or repetition, is a something public speakers sometimes do to get the audience's attention and drive a point home.

So let freedom ring from the prodigious [remarkable] hilltops of New Hampshire. Let freedom ring from the mighty mountains of New York. Let freedom ring from the heightening Alleghenies of Pennsylvania! Let freedom ring from the snowcapped Rockies of Colorado! Let freedom ring from the curvaceous peaks of California! But not only that; let freedom ring from Stone Mountain of Georgia! Let freedom ring from Lookout Mountain of Tennessee! Let freedom ring from every hill and every molehill of Mississippi. From every mountainside, let freedom ring.

One part of Stone Mountain Georgia contains a granite carving honoring the Confederacy. The carving had been started, but not completed, by the time of King's speech.

Free at last

And he ends the speech with a paragraph ending in perhaps the most famous lines King ever spoke:

When we let freedom ring, when we let it ring from every village and every hamlet, from every state and every city, we will be able to speed up that day when all of God's children, black men and white men, Jews and Gentiles, Protestants and Catholics, will be able to join hands and sing in the words of the old Negro spiritual, "Free at last! free at last! Thank God Almighty, we are free at last!"

Know It!

John Lewis, a young representative from a **civil rights** group called Student Nonviolent Coordinating Committee, also spoke to the crowd on August 28, 1963. In his speech, Lewis said, "For those who have said, 'Be patient and wait!' we must say, 'Patience is a dirty and nasty word.' We cannot be patient, we do not want to be free gradually, we want our freedom, and we want it now." In 1986 John Lewis was elected to the United States House of Representatives to represent his state of Georgia.

John Lewis, seen here at the March on Washington, is the son of sharecroppers. Today he serves as a member of the U.S. Congress.

A First-Hand Account

In his autobiography, King wrote that the March on Washington marked the first time the American news media paid so much attention to something African Americans did. For many Americans, this was the first time they had heard King speak. It was the first time some realized that a black person could express such serious, intelligent thoughts. King wrote that on August 28, 1963, that after the March on Washington, "The **stereotype** of the Negro suffered a heavy blow." The march also provided an example to the world of the American idea of peaceful demonstration.

George Raveling

One young man who was standing on the platform while King delivered his speech was George Raveling. He had just ended four years as an outstanding college basketball player and later had a thirty-year career as a professional basketball coach. He had driven to the march with his best friend, and just before the march they were asked to help out as volunteer security guards.

While he was protecting King on the platform, Raveling noticed that, as King spoke, he left the text he had prepared and began saying the phrase "I have a dream." The words of the speech were made public before the speech—King had given out copies to newspapers so they could publish the speech after he gave it.

George Raveling (seen here in 1983) was on the podium during King's speech.

Raveling said:

> As he began delivering the prepared text, he saw that it was really capturing the crowd. That's when [gospel singer] Mahalia Jackson began egging him on. If you listen carefully to the speech you can hear a woman's voice in the back say, 'Please, Martin, tell them about the dream.' She was saying it constantly. It was like going to church on Sunday at a black church and people are making little remarks. From that point on he didn't read the speech, he only used it as a guidepost.

When King ended his speech, he waved goodbye to the crowd and began to walk off. Raveling stepped forward and asked King if he could have King's copy. King handed the pages to him. Then another man spoke to King, and he turned away. Raveling still has the typewritten pages.

Mahalia Jackson

Mahalia Jackson was born in New Orleans in 1911. She began recording gospel albums in the 1930s. In 1946 her recording of "Move On Up a Little Higher" sold more than 2 million copies. The sales earned her the nickname "The Gospel Queen." By 1954 she had her own radio and television programs. Jackson was very involved in the Civil Rights Movement and she sang at the March on Washington. Jackson died in 1972.

Mahalia Jackson was famous as a civil rights leader and a gospel singer.

The Violence Continues

Not long after the March on Washington, a tragedy occurred in Birmingham, Alabama. Schools were to be integrated starting in September 1963. But Governor George Wallace disagreed so strongly with **integration** that he ordered the schools closed rather than allowing it. President Kennedy had to step in to keep the schools open.

Church bombing

On September 15, a bomb exploded at the Sixteenth Street Baptist Church in Birmingham. Four young black girls, who were in the church basement, getting ready for Sunday school, were killed. When the news spread, riots broke out in Birmingham. Many blacks tried to calm things down, asking for peace. But people were so angry at the injustice that they saw no other way to respond.

The deaths of the four girls brought more attention to the problems between whites and blacks. President Kennedy began to focus more attention on his **civil rights** bill. But before he could see it made into law, he was **assassinated**. On November 22, 1963, he was shot while riding through Dallas, Texas.

The site of the devestating Birmingham church bombing.

36

Lyndon Johnson is sworn in as president after Kennedy's assasination.

Kennedy's death shocked all Americans. African Americans saw him as someone who would work for their rights, and they wondered what the new president, Lyndon B. Johnson, would do. But Johnson knew how important Kennedy's civil rights act was. He persuaded Congress to pass the bill, and in 1964 the Civil Rights Act became law. The act made **discrimination** against people because of race, color, religion, or national origin illegal.

Even with this new law, discrimination continued. In some parts of the South, whites were trying to stop blacks from voting. Some places even forced blacks to take a test proving they could read and write before they were allowed to vote. States such as Mississippi passed laws that went against the Civil Rights Act and that were designed to keep blacks from voting.

To help blacks register to vote and educate them about voting rights, a group of volunteers traveled to Mississippi during the summer of 1964. Some whites fought against anyone who tried to help the blacks, bombing homes, burning churches, and beating them. One day, three young volunteers disappeared. **Federal** agents traveled to Mississippi to investigate and found their bodies. The young men had been kidnapped and murdered. More than twenty people were charged with the murders, including some police officers.

Selma to Montgomery

The campaign to get African Americans to register to vote continued in Selma, Alabama. Half of the people who lived in Selma, Alabama, were African American. But only a handful of those people were registered to vote. One reason was Jim Crow laws. Blacks who tried to vote in Selma were often stopped by police or even by the officials in charge of the voting stations. Sometimes, black voters were forced to pay a tax to be able to vote. Many of the blacks in Selma felt so discouraged—or afraid—that they did not want to register.

Voter registration drive

In January 1965 two **civil rights** groups, the Student Nonviolent Coordinating Committee and the Southern Christian Leadership Council, decided to travel to Selma to get blacks to register to vote. Martin Luther King Jr., went to Selma to lend his support.

The civil rights workers marched through the streets of Selma, encouraging blacks to register to vote. Often, they sang as they marched, and sometimes they stopped to pray. The sheriff did not want the protesters in his city, and he arrested those he said got too close to the courthouse. King was one of the 2,000 people who were arrested.

Long lines of African Americans wait to register to vote in Alabama.

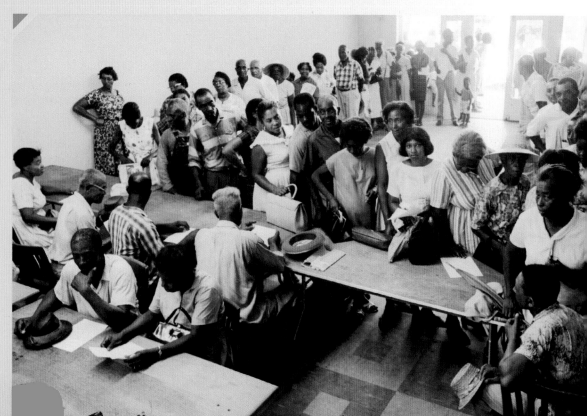

Police line up to stop a civil rights march in Selma.

After they were released from jail, King and other leaders decided to organize a 54-mile-long march from Selma to Montgomery, Alabama's capital. In Montgomery, the marchers planned to meet with politicians to discuss the problems blacks were having with voting in Selma. They also planned to demand changes in laws so the problems in Selma would end.

Attempting to march

Five hundred people started the march on March 7, 1965, but only 300 yards into their journey they were stopped by police. The leaders asked the local court to review the facts and allow them to march without harassment from the police. The judge agreed to review the facts and make a decision in a few days. But the marchers were eager to practice their right of peaceful protest, so they attempted to march again on March 9. Again, they were stopped by police, and one protester was beaten to death by local whites.

President Johnson closely watched events in Selma. Johnson was planning to present a new voting rights bill to **Congress**. He voiced his support of the protestors in a televised speech to Congress on March 15.

The March for Civil Rights

O n March 17 the judge announced his decision. He said that the march "is clearly a reasonable exercise of a right guaranteed by the Constitution of the United States." Governor George Wallace protested that the state did not have the money to pay for all the security it would take to guard the marchers, but President Johnson responded by ordering federal troops and law enforcement officers into the city.

The march

The march officially began on March 21 with 3,000 marchers. Dr. Martin Luther King Jr., walked at the front. When they approached Montgomery on the 24th, 10,000 more joined them. More people came from all over the country, until the ranks swelled to 25,000. The march was organized and peaceful.

President Johnson was already planning to present the voting rights bill to **Congress**, but the peaceful but determined demonstration influenced Congress, as well. On August 6, Congress passed the Voting Rights Act of 1965.

The march also encouraged blacks to register to vote. In Mississippi, for example, the number of blacks registered to vote increased from 7 percent to 67 percent, or two-thirds of blacks who were eligible.

The beginning of the march in Alabama.

George Wallace delivering his "Segregation Now" inauguration speech.

Governor George Wallace (1919–1998)

George Wallace is an intriguing and confusing political figure. He was born in rural Alabama in 1919. He first ran for governor of Alabama in 1958. During this race his opponent accepted the help of the Ku Klux Klan. Wallace refused to be supported by the KKK and won the endorsement of the NAACP. Wallace lost the election. After his defeat, Wallace's views on race changed drastically. The next time he ran for governor, in 1962 he received the greatest number of votes of any candidate for Alabama governor at the time. In his **inauguration** address Wallace quoted the Confederate general, Robert E. Lee, and referenced the Confederate president, Jefferson Davis. The most famous line from this speech is "Segregation today…segregation tomorrow…segregation forever."

For many, Wallace became a symbol of racism. However, when Wallace ran for governor in 1982 he received an unprecedented amount of black voter support. Wallace was governor of Alabama four times. He died in 1998.

Know It!

Part of the United States Constitution is called The Bill of Rights. It says that Congress will make no law against "the right of the people to peaceably assemble." This is what the protesters in Selma asked the judge to consider in 1965. He agreed that the marchers had this right, and that they could go ahead with the march.

King Assassinated

For the next few years, King continued **civil rights** work. In April 1968, he traveled to Memphis, Tennessee, to support a **strike** by city garbage workers. On April 3, King gave what would be his final speech. Called "I See the Promised Land," he made the speech to some of the garbage workers and local civil rights activists. In the speech, King said, "I've seen the promised land. [But] I may not get there with you." By this he meant that he knew a better day was coming for black people in America.

Many were surprised to hear King say this. He was only 39. Did he mean that after all the work they had done in their struggle for civil rights—for freedom—that the "promised land" was still many years in the future?

His words proved tragically accurate.

This is the sanitation worker's strike King was attending when he was assasinated.

The site of King's assasination quickly became a shrine to King.

Assassinated

On the afternoon of April 4, the day after he made his speech, King spent some time in his hotel room, then decided to go to dinner at about 5 o'clock. As soon as he opened the door and stepped out onto the balcony, he was shot. Not long after he was taken to the hospital, he died.

The man who shot King was James Earl Ray. He had been following King, and he rented a room in a building across from the room where King was staying. After the murder, Ray escaped to England. He was captured two months later, found guilty of the murder, and given a 99-year prison term. He died in prison in 1998.

Before he died, Ray insisted that he was not guilty. King's family believed Ray and was convinced that King's death was the result of a **conspiracy**.

Know It!

Today, a museum is on the site of the hotel where King was **assassinated** in Memphis called the National Civil Rights Museum. About 150,000 people visit the museum each year.

The Legacy of "I Have a Dream"

Dr. Martin Luther King Jr., is considered a hero by many people. They admire the courage he showed as he led the struggle for civil rights. They praise his leadership ability and the intelligence he demonstrated in his speeches and written words.

Some people, however, believe King could have done more to further the cause of **civil rights**. They feel his peaceful, nonviolent approach to fighting against **racism** slowed down the progress of the civil rights movement.

The King Center

King's life and work are honored by the center his family established in his name. The King Center is in Atlanta, Georgia. More than half a million people visit the center each year. In the center are exhibits about King's life and teachings. A library, King's birthplace and grave, and a gift shop are included at the center. Papers, books, and audio and video tapes relating to King are stored in an archive there.

The Martin Luther King Jr. Center for Nonviolent Social Change in Atlanta, Georgia.

This memorial to King is located in Atlanta.

Martin Luther King Jr. was one of the most inspiring and influential people in American history. His legacy is broad. Through his dignity, intellect, and love he led the way for many to the "promised land."

Martin Luther King Jr. Day

In 1968 after Martin Luther King Jr. was **assassinated**, a senator from Michigan introduced the idea of a holiday to honor him. Little action was taken to make the day official, but later a petition with 6,000,000 signatures of people who wanted the holiday was presented to **Congress**. In 1983 Congress agreed to make King's birthday, January 15, an official federal holiday. Congress decided to declare the official holiday as the third Monday in January. By 1999 all fifty states had adopted the holiday.

Glossary

abolitionists people who worked to end slavery

assassination murder, especially of a political leader

autobiography story of someone's life, written by that person

boycott refusal to do business with or engage in other activities with a person, business, organization, or government

civil rights claims of personal liberty guaranteed to United States citizens by the Constitution and by acts of Congress

Congress law-making body of the United States government

conspiracy secret plot, often involving the government

desegregate stop separating people based on race

discrimination unfair treatment of a person because of their race, religion, gender, or other reason

draft unfinished form of a piece of writing

federal one central government that oversees smaller units; the smaller units, such as states, have their own governments

inauguration ceremony that gives a person a new position

integration to bring people, things, or ideas together; racial integration is when people of all races mix together in schools, organizations, businesses, and neighborhoods

legislature law-making section of a government

lynch illegal group action resulting in a person's death, usually by hanging

racism idea that one race is superior to another

segregation forced separation of people of different races

stereotype idea that all people who look one way or belong to a particular group will act in an expected way

strike method used by workers of stopping work to get attention of management

Supreme Court highest court in the United States

More Books to Read

Downing, David. *Leading Lives: Martin Luther King Jr.* Chicago: Heinemann Library, 2002.

King, Christine Farris. *My Brother Martin: A Sister Remembers Growing Up with the Rev. Dr. Martin Luther King Jr.* New York: Simon & Schuster Children's Publisher, 2003.

Places to Visit

The King Center
449 Auburn Avenue, NE
Atlanta, Ga 30312
(404) 526-8900

National Civil Rights Museum
450 Mulberry Street
Memphis, TN 38103
(901) 521-9699

Index